IRISH TRACTION
IARNRÓD ÉIREANN

Colm O'Callaghan

AMBERLEY

With the collapse of the Cahir viaduct on the Limerick Junction to Waterford line in October 2003, at the start of the sugar beet harvesting campaign, all sugar beet traffic was diverted from Waterford to Kildare on the Cork mainline to Mallow. 201 Class locomotives were never used on freight traffic on the Limerick Junction to Waterford line, but worked regularly on the diverted beet trains via Kildare. 201 Class No. 211 arrives at Cherryville Junction with the 7.45 laden sugar beet on Wednesday 12 November 2003.

Front Cover: A Class locomotive No. 051 is departing Mosney after being signal checked with the midday 12.15 Adelaide (Belfast) to North Wall (Dublin) freightliner train on Wednesday 15 July 1992. Although the Great Northern Railway (Ireland) had been dissolved thirty-three years previously, Mosney retained a fine collection of that company's lower-quadrant semaphore signals right until the end of mechanical signalling on this section of the Dublin–Drogheda line in May 1994. The loop at Mosney was disconnected and taken out of use on 26 June 2015.

Rear Cover: Triple power – well, not quite! On Monday 26 May 2003, 181 Class locomotive No. 184 had failed on the North Wall to Heuston Guinness keg transfer at North Strand Junction, so sister engines Nos 146 and 156 came off an engineers' train in Connolly station to rescue the stricken keg train. The three locomotives, with No. 146 taking the lead, are pictured approaching the footbridge at Claude Road near Drumcondra, in Dublin City's north inner suburbs, en route to the freight yard near Heuston station.

First published 2019

Amberley Publishing
The Hill, Stroud
Gloucestershire, GL5 4EP

www.amberley-books.com

Copyright © Colm O'Callaghan, 2019

The right of Colm O'Callaghan to be identified as the Author of this work has been asserted in accordance with the Copyrights, Designs and Patents Act 1988.

ISBN 978 1 4456 8844 2 (print)
ISBN 978 1 4456 8845 9 (ebook)

British Library Cataloguing in Publication Data. A catalogue record for this book is available from the British Library.

Typesetting by Aura Technology and Software Services, India. Printed in the UK.

Introduction

Apart from my two grandfathers working in the railway, I have no other family connections with rail transport. While one could say the railways run in my blood, the link was tenuous at best, and of my own generation, none ever showed any desire to follow in the footsteps of my grandfathers. Growing up in Finglas, where I am still resident to this day, I could not claim my interest was stimulated by visits to a local railway station, this Dublin suburb being far from any railway line and firmly served by a principal bus corridor leading from the north of the city, although there is always talk of a metro being built. So the environment where many railway enthusiasts found their origins simply did not exist for me.

Writing now in 2019, after hundreds of miles clocked up travelling and photographing railways in Ireland and in recent years abroad, my interest in rail transport and their history, I can claim, now spans nearly forty years. However, there were flickering signs even before then that I would be inevitably be drawn towards the railway – not deliberately, it has to be said, but more so by the personal circumstances which brought me into both the sight and contact of that form of transport.

The earliest significant memory I have of the railways that I can trace goes back to my school days where, in the early 1960s, I attended St Vincent's CBS at Glasnevin, located in the outskirts of inner Dublin City. Then as now, the school's southern boundary adjoins the busy Glasnevin Junction, where two lines leading into Dublin and its port converge. Looking from the windows of my classroom on the second floor and across the sports fields, the railway line could be glimpsed beyond the wall. What fascinated me was the North City Mill on the southern side of the tracks, whose premises were served by a siding adjacent to the junction. This siding was, in effect, a short branch line that extended from Liffey Junction, located further west off the Galway and Sligo line. A Metrovick locomotive, of which I knew little then, would propel back from Liffey Junction to the North City Mill and shunt loose coupled wagons into the mill over a small bridge at the Sixth Lock on the Royal Canal, and all this I could see from the classroom. Years later I would learn from my senior railway photographers just how challenging and satisfying it was to record the elusive workings to the North City Mills, something which in the years ahead I grew fully to understand and appreciate during my own 'gricing' expeditions.

With the closure of the North City Mill siding in the early 1970s, and later leaving school to work in the Posts & Telegraph, I once again came into contact with the railways. This time it was in the form of the mail trains, whereby I was travelling out to Dún Laoghaire Pier and meeting the 'mail boat' trains that would arrive from Dublin's Connolly station, from which I returned to the city centre in my van laden with registered post. When Dún Laoghaire Pier, or Carlisle Pier as it was sometimes known, closed to rail traffic in 1980, I immediately regretted the fact that I had not recorded the everyday scene that I so closely participated in. This regret proved to be the great impetus that led me to purchase my first camera and from then on I set out to record the Irish railway scene, in the knowledge that railways are forever changing. I particularly looked up to fellow enthusiasts and photographers, such as modest individuals like the late Joe St Leger of Cork, and David Boyle of Dublin, who recorded everything on the railways no matter how great or little its significance was; they were my mentors and we became great friends. Both men have now since passed on, but their legacy is still revered and appreciated by all with a genuine interest in Irish railways.

In 1982, my interest in the railway scene was further stimulated when I joined the Irish Railway Record Society and upon purchasing the aforementioned camera, this started a life-long hobby recording daily events on the railway, along with meeting new, likeminded friends in the Society who shared my passion. I travelled throughout Ireland with these friends, such as Alan Keller, who was my regular companion during the 1990s. We travelled everywhere to places of railway interest, and in recent years, my long suffering friend Richard Wall is now a regular companion, as well as numerous other photographers who I developed a close, life-long companionship with over the years; these include John Cleary, Aidan McDonnell, Mark Hodge and Barry Carse, some of whom had been photographing the railways well before I started. Now, with new friendships in younger enthusiasts Ciarán Cooney and Shane Roberts, the hobby is passing on to the next generation.

Of the huge changes that have occurred on Irish railways, which I have recorded over the preceding the years, the most significant was the dramatic decline in the variety of rail freight traffic, where nowadays freight is largely concentrated on one individual large container customer, with timber and ore traffic representing the other flows still existing. The other big transformation to occur on the railways was the move from locomotive-hauled passenger trains to DMU operation (or railcars as they are generally known in Ireland). Traditional signal-controlled lines with their signal boxes and semaphores have also significantly contracted with the widespread introduction of modern colour-light signals and Centralised Traffic Control. I recorded the above changes over a period of thirty years and some of these are illustrated in the following pages. For readers wishing to learn more about the historic developments of Ireland's railway system, I recommend the *Journal of the Irish Railway Record Society*, which since 1947 have chronicled in great detail all aspects of Irish railway infrastructure and operations. In addition, the *Irish Railways Traction & Travel* book, published by the Irish Traction Group, details the profiles of Irish locomotive and railcar classes past and present, many of which are illustrated in this book.

Meeting many railway people over the years, I would particularly like to thank Larry Oglesby, Station Inspector in Dublin's Connolly station, Inspector John Belton of the Holyhead Yard in North Wall, Train Examiner Tony Maguire of the Midland Yard, as well as Inspector Willie Hogan in the Point Yard, both also based in North Wall, Dublin. In addition, Foreman Rory O'Conor in North Wall's wagon shop and Paschal Reddin of Portlaoise, both of whom have always been a great help to me over many years in recording the latest happenings on the railway scene.

A special thanks must go to Ciarán Cooney, Hon. Photographic Archivist of the Irish Railway Record Society, for his expert advice and assistance in selecting the images, which turned out to be a huge task, retrieving thousands of my 35 mm slides, and also in digitising some of the more difficult images in order to produce their best quality for light and colour balance. Ciarán's assistance and expertise in this area was invaluable, as was his knowledge of Irish railway history which greatly enhanced the accompanying photo captions. Finally to my wife Anne, and my two daughters Deirdre and Siobhán, a big 'Thank You' for being so understanding in my pursuit of this crazy but greatly rewarding hobby.

Ireland's first railway started here at Dublin's Westland Row station, when an 8½-mile line of 4 foot 8½ inch track opened to Kingstown (Dún Laoghaire) in October 1834. The line was later converted to the standard Irish gauge of 5 feet 3 inches in 1857. Renamed Pearse station in 1966, NIR locomotive No. 111 is passing through the city centre station en route to the 'Boston Yard' to run-round with the 11.35 Cabra to Platin Cement Factory empty bulk cement train on Sunday 22 February 1998.

Much of the former Dublin & South Eastern Railway hugs the coastline, which leads to many scenic stretches of line for photography. Pictured at White Rock, near Killiney, is locomotive No. 048, which is working the 9.40 Shelton Abbey to Marino Point empty ammonia on Sunday 17 May 1992. This area of the coast has been known by Dubliners as the 'Bay of Naples'.

On Friday 14 June 1996, 071 Class locomotive No. 086 is at White Rock with the morning 6.57 Arklow to Dublin Connolly passenger service. Down below to the left is Killiney Beach and in the background is the single-storey house belonging to the original Killiney station, which opened first with the line in 1858 and was replaced by the present day Killiney & Ballybrack station in May 1882.

Class leader locomotive No. 071 departs Bray with the 15.00 Rosslare Harbour to Dublin Connolly passenger service on Monday 29 May 1995. Behind the train can be glimpsed an electrified DART train entering the station. 2700 Class diesel railcars displaced 071 Class locomotives from Rosslare trains in 2003. Looming large on the horizon above the town is Bray Head, which the railway navigates via a cliff edge cut into the head in order to continue south to Greystones and beyond.

Locomotives Nos 135 and 131 are negotiating the line around Bray Head with the 5.30 laden Tara Mines (Navan) zinc ore train, which had stabled overnight at Pearse station, en route to the port of Arklow for export on Saturday 27 June 1992. This working was a trial run utilising 20-foot containers with tarpaulin covers and only lasted for six weeks during the summer of 1992. The zinc flow from the mines at Navan reverted back to Dublin Port, where they continue to operate to this present day, albeit with the standard ore wagons dating from flow's commencement in 1977.

141 Class locomotive No. 158 has just passed the disused platform of Naylor's Cove halt at Bray Head with DART sets 8119 and 8319, working from Bray to Greystones on a publicity launch on Monday 29 May 1995. An announcement was made in Greystones on the day by the Minister for Transport (TD Michael Lowry) on the electrification of the Bray–Greystones section. The DART service from Bray to Greystones commenced operating in April 2000. Opened in 1908 and closed in 1926, the short platform at Naylor's Cove was primarily used by bathers accessing the small rocky inlet from which the halt took its name.

201 Class locomotive No. 220 travels down the east coast at Bray Head with the 8.42 Marino Point to Shelton Abbey laden ammonia train on Monday 26 June 1995. The construction of the railway around Bray Head to Greystones was planned and executed by the famous British engineer Isambard Kingdom Brunel. The 1855-built line featured examples of the engineer's wooden trestle viaducts, as well as several tunnels. This part of the line is susceptible to coastal erosion and several sections of Brunel's original route, including his viaducts, have been removed or altered to avoid many of its defects, leading Bray Head to acquire the nickname 'Brunel's Folly'.

C Class locomotive No. 213 waits to depart Greystones with the Bray to Greystones shuttle service on Saturday 10 May 1986. This service operated primarily for passengers wishing to connect with DART services to and from Dublin City. This shuttle provided one of the last regular passenger workings for the former Metrovick C Class locomotives, which eked out much of their remaining duties on Dublin suburban trains prior to the DART electrification in 1984. Delivered to CIÉ from Metropolitan Vickers in 1957 for the purpose of branch line and suburban work, their underpowered 550 hp Crossley engines were replaced by 1,100 hp GM engines between 1969 and 1972. All were withdrawn by the close of 1988.

Locomotive No. 048 is recorded passing the single-platform station at Kilcoole with the 9.35 Dublin Connolly to Rosslare Harbour passenger on Saturday 8 September 1990. To the left can be seen the Sugarloaf Mountain, part of the scenic County Wicklow mountain range. This 10-mile section of line between Bray and Wicklow features the straightest and most level stretch of railway in Ireland. During the 1980s and 1990s, the small village of Kilcoole starred in Ireland's television drama series *Glenroe*.

Locomotive No. 169 is departing from the Down siding at Enniscorthy with a laden ballast train for Wellington Bridge on the South Wexford line on Saturday 8 August 1998. As was the normal practice with ballast workings on Irish Rail, a guard's van, complete with underframe plough, is positioned at the front and rear of the train. These wagons and vans were introduced to traffic in 1972 and 1977 respectively and remained in traffic until May 2013, when they were completely displaced by the then recently introduced HOBS wagon fleet.

On Monday 26 August 1991, locomotive No. 047 heads through the forlorn-looking station at Ferns with a Platin to Wexford bag cement train, which called at Arklow, Gorey, Enniscorthy and Wexford. Ferns closed to passenger traffic in 1964 and to goods in March 1977, one of the latter traffics being tar, where tank wagons were loaded and unloaded from a siding which formerly existed on the left.

141 Class locomotive No. 163 has just passed the former station of Wexford South with the 12.30 Wexford to Waterford empty bag cement on Saturday 8 August 1998. When Arklow, Gorey and Enniscorthy closed to bag traffic, these trains for Wexford operated from Waterford via the South Wexford Line. This section of line was formerly a branch from Rosslare Strand, but these days it forms part of the main line from Dublin Connolly to Rosslare Europort. Wexford South station was closed in 1977.

Locomotive No. 038 is arriving at Rosslare Strand with the 9.35 Dublin Connolly to Rosslare Harbour passenger train on Friday 30 August 1991. In August 1906, Rosslare Strand became a junction station for the South Wexford Line from Waterford. The construction of the line to Waterford was a joint venture between the Great Southern & Western Railway of Ireland and the English Great Western Railway, under the title of the Fishguard & Rosslare Railways & Harbours Company, and was primarily used as a means to speed up the transit of mails between Rosslare Harbour and the port of Cobh in County Cork.

Locomotive No. 076 enters Rosslare Strand with the diverted Platin to Waterford bulk cement train, consisting of the four-wheel cement 'bubble' wagons, on Wednesday 21 April 2004. This train would have departed Dublin's North Wall yard at 9.30, arriving at Rosslare Strand to run round its train and depart for Waterford. Although the importance of the South Wexford Line had declined significantly by 2004, note how the semaphore arms of the junction signal indicate the Waterford line as the 'main line' and the Wexford line as the 'branch'.

121 Class locomotives Nos 132 and 121 descend the gradient from Kilrane and enter Rosslare Europort with the 9.35 passenger train from Dublin Connolly on Tuesday 28 July 1992. Locomotive No. 132 is sporting the new bright red day-glow panels, which were neatly applied to the front and rear of Irish Rail's locomotive fleet. The line in the foreground formerly led from the goods yard, locomotive shed and turntable, but the only the last remains in use today.

On Saturday 24 June 1989, locomotive No. 005 accelerates out of Rosslare Europort with the afternoon 14.55 passenger service to Dublin Connolly. In the background to the right of the photo is the RPSI's 2-6-4T locomotive No. 4 (ex-LMS NCC of Derby, built 1947), which can be seen emerging from the turntable siding to work the return 'Sea Breeze' steam special to Dublin.

Locomotives Nos 127 and 129 are recorded at Wellington Bridge, adjacent to the sugar beet loading facility, on Wednesday 8 November 1995. This beet loading facility was opened for the 1980 beet campaign and was received by beet growers throughout south County Wexford. Upon completion of loading, the train would depart for Waterford and onwards to the sugar factory at Mallow, County Cork. The conveyance of this beet traffic finished in January 2006, and with it was the last important traffic flow to be carried over the Waterford–Rosslare Harbour line.

Locomotive No. 163 is at Wellington Bridge working the 9.00 Waterford to Wexford bag cement train on Saturday 8 August 1998. Visible behind the station building is a laden ballast train waiting to enter the Wellington Bridge–Waterford section. Note how some of the side doors of the cement wagons have been replaced by curtains, a feature common to these wagons in their latter years.

Locomotives Nos 185 and 124 have just crossed the seven-arch viaduct at Taylorstown on the South Wexford Line with a diverted Platin to Waterford bulk cement train on Friday 24 September 2004. The brick-built viaduct at Taylorstown was destroyed during the Irish Civil War in July 1922, and consequently the South Wexford Line did not reopen fully until January the following year, when the damaged arches were rebuilt.

141 Class locomotives working in multiple were a common feature of beet trains from the mid-1990s onward. Here locomotives Nos 146 and 142 climb the steep 1-in-30 gradient from Taylorstown to Ballycullane with the 15.00 Wellington Bridge to Mallow Beet Factory laden beet on Saturday 2 November 2003. Entering service with CIÉ in December 1962, No. 146 is now preserved in running order at the Downpatrick & County Down Railway and is owned by the Irish Traction Group (ITG), having been taken out of service in 2010.

Resplendent in the then new black and silver livery, the 071 Class leader, No. 071, passes the bare-looking Ballycullane station with an empty ballast train following the discharge of its load near Wellington Bridge on Thursday 16 October 2008. The one-time island platform at Ballycullane formerly boasted station buildings, signal cabin and footbridge, but all were gradually removed following the closure of the signal cabin and block-post in autumn 1980.

Pictured from the twelfth-century Dunbrody Abbey, west of Campile, on Saturday 19 October 1991, A Class locomotive No. 055 is recorded with a laden beet working from Wellington Bridge to Mallow beet factory. A key obtained from a local cottage allowed access to the top of the abbey. Taken out of service in 1995, No. 055 is now preserved as a static exhibit at the Castlerea Railway Museum, County Roscommon.

Locomotive No. 038 approaches Belview with a laden beet working from Wellington Bridge to Mallow beet factory on Saturday 10 October 1992. The train would shortly pass the construction site for the extensive Belview Port, which opened for business in 1993. In the background can be seen huge excavation work in association with the creation of a temporary road adjacent to the railway for the port's construction traffic.

Locomotives Nos 141 and 169 stand in Waterford's Sally Park yard with an empty timber train on Saturday 1 October 2005. The doyen of the 141 Class locomotives, No. 141, is now preserved by the Railway Preservation Society of Ireland (RPSI). To the right is the Irish Cement Ltd silo, which received bulk cement from Limerick and Platin, but which ceased operation in 2009.

Locomotive No. 081 is pictured within Belview Port loading a Norfolk Liner train on Thursday 16 October 2008. Belview Port opened for business in 1993. Since the demise of the Bell Lines traffic in 1997, different shipping companies have operated liner trains from Belview Port, including Andrew Weir Shipping (AWS), Norfolk Lines and, in more recent years, DFDS. Imported steel rails are also unloaded at Belview for onward transit to Iarnród Éireann's principal engineering base at Portlaoise, Co. Laois.

In autumn light, the driver of locomotive No. 051 prepares to exchange staffs at Carrick-On-Suir with the 10.15 Mallow to Waterford empty beet on Saturday 22 October 1993. Carrick-On-Suir is a base and workshop for the Irish Traction Group and two of their locomotives can be seen outside the shed, these being ex-CIÉ C Class No. 231 and Sulzer engine No. B103. Locomotive No. 231 also now resides at the preserved Downpatrick & County Down Railway, where she has been restored to her original 1957 green livery.

By then, the last surviving pair of the 121 Class fleet, Nos 124 and 134 are recorded west of Carrick-On-Suir with the 12.00 Waterford to Limerick cement factory (Castlemungret) empty bulk cement train on Friday 2 March 2007. Both these locomotives continued in service until early 2008, the majority of the fleet having been withdrawn from service seven years previously. No. 124 is now preserved by the ITG and currently resides at the West Clare Railway, Moyasta, County Clare, while at the time of writing sister locomotive No. 134 is currently being restored to running order by the RPSI at Inchicore Works, Dublin.

Locomotives Nos 150 and 162 catch the winter light between Clonmel and Kilsheelan with the morning 8.30 Mallow to Waterford empty beet working during a very late sugar beet campaign season on Tuesday 15 January 2002. These four-wheel wagons used on the beet trains were originally constructed during the 1950s, but their capacity were doubled in size in the mid-1980s when two wagon bodies were placed one on top of the other. At the same time, the wagons were equipped with vacuum brakes, which removed the need for brake vans.

Locomotives Nos 185 and 175 round the curve at Nicholastown with the 9.10 Wellington Bridge to Mallow beet factory with the 'new look' sugar beet bogie container wagons on Saturday 19 November 2005. Regrettably, these new wagons only worked one beet campaign, the final campaign, as Greencore exited the business, which resulted in the closure of the last remaining sugar beet factory in Ireland in May 2006, after seventy-seven years of sugar beet harvest in Ireland. On the horizon in the far distance is the 721-metre (2,365 ft) Slievenamon Mountain in County Tipperary.

Locomotives Nos 175 and 128 depart from Tipperary with the 11.30 Waterford to Mallow beet factory laden beet on Saturday 8 December 2001. Up to the time of writing Tipperary still has a working signal box (or cabin, as is the common term on Irish railways) with a twenty-one-lever frame and ETS instrument with tokens.

Locomotive No. 148 is pictured east of Killonan with the 11.47 Limerick to Limerick Junction shuttle service on Tuesday 18 March 2003. The train is formed of two CIÉ Craven coaches and a British Railways-built Mk I steam generator van (GSV).

Class leader No. 141 is departing Limerick and passing Limerick Check with the 15.10 Limerick to Limerick Junction shuttle on Thursday 1 April 1999. It is known as 'Limerick Check' because the former 'Check Platform' was located here, adjacent to the signal cabin, which was used for ticket inspections of incoming trains. Diverging to the left behind the cabin is the Foynes branch, which closed in 2000. Straight ahead are two locomotives outside Limerick shed. Limerick Check cabin closed in June 2017 when the Limerick station area was re-signalled.

A Class locomotive No. 054 enters Birdhill with the Limerick to Roscrea liner train on Wednesday 18 July 1990. Both the shale siding at Kilmastulla and the junction ground frame release for the Silvermines branch were controlled remotely from Birdhill cabin. Until 1947, the Up platform at Birdhill was used by trains for the short branch line to Killaloe, which diverged just north of the station.

181 Class locomotive No. 184 heads out of Roscrea with the 19.08 evening train from Ballybrophy to Limerick on Saturday 9 June 1990. The trackbed in the foreground beside the train is the remains of the branch line to Birr, which closed in December 1962. This branch ran alongside the Limerick line for nearly a mile before diverging north for Birr.

On Monday 19 May 1997, locomotive No. 144 is recorded in Roscrea yard unloading a bag cement train, which it had worked earlier from Limerick that morning, dropping off thirteen wagons in Nenagh. Roscrea still has a working signal cabin with twenty-four levers and an ETS instrument for tokens.

Locomotive No. 039 is starting the climb up the Silvermines branch with an empty barytes working from the port of Foynes on a warm summer's day on Wednesday 18 July 1990. The level crossing in the foreground is the Shalee Road gates. Locomotive No. 039 is preserved as 'A39' by the Irish Traction Group (ITG) in running order at the Downpatrick & County Down Railway, County Down.

Locomotives Nos 189 and 160 pass through Athy with the Galway to Waterford laden timber train on Monday 20 April 1998. At the time of writing, timber traffic can still be seen regularly passing through Athy station, en route from Ballina to Waterford. South of the station, the now disused Wolfhill branch diverges west to the Tegral factory.

Locomotives Nos 157 and 129 cross the River Barrow in Athy on the Tegral factory line, formerly the 'goods-only' Wolfhill branch, with the 12.50 Tegral factory to Limerick cement factory empty bulk cement train on Friday 19 April 2002.

Northern Ireland Railways (NIR) locomotive No. 208 is departing south from Athy station with the 11.30 Heuston to Waterford (Plunkett) passenger service, formed of Mk III stock, on Thursday 17 October 1996. In the background, the Wolfhill branch can be glimpsed diverging from the left with a traditional type semaphore signal protecting its entry into the station. This branch line has not seen regular traffic since 2003 and, at the time of writing of writing in March 2019, has now been issued with a formal 'abandonment order'.

Locomotives Nos 131 and 122 depart from the loop at Carlow with the 4.00 Limerick to Waterford diverted Ennis timber train having been overtaken by the 7.40 Heuston to Waterford Plunkett passenger service on Tuesday 30 March 1999. The four-wheel timber wagons used on these trains ceased operation in 2001 following the initial withdrawal of timber traffic on Irish Rail. Only the bogie timber wagons remain in use on the timber trains.

Locomotive No. 233 departs Muine Bheag (Bagenalstown) with the 11.30 Dublin Heuston to Waterford (Plunkett) passenger service on Monday 1 February 1999. Until April 1963, the former 24-mile branch line from Place East used to converge from the right and terminate in a bay platform on the Down side of the station, the remnants of which can be seen in the distance beside the locomotive working north 'light-engine'. Although the branch line lost its regular passenger and goods services in 1931 and 1947 respectively, it remained in regular use for the seasonal sugar beet traffic and occasional GAA excursion trains.

Locomotives Nos 122 and 141 are on the freight-only Alexandra Road 'tramway' with the empty Acrylonitrile tanks, en route to the Asahi Terminal in Dublin Port on Thursday 9 October 1997. This tank traffic came to an end with the closure of the Asahi plant in Killala, County Mayo, in November 1997.

Class leader No. 071, recorded just before receiving its retro-style CIÉ livery, arrives at Alexandra Road with the 9.20 Navan to Alexandra Road Tara mines ore train (designated code M103) on Wednesday 30 March 2016. This stretch of the tramway remains busy, Monday–Friday, with the Tara mines and IWT liner trains.

Freshly repainted locomotive No. 145 is recorded at the Coastal Siding on the Alexandra Road Extension on Thursday 30 April 1998. The Coastal Siding opened for container traffic in March 1998 and closed at the end of 2001, when the Coastal Containers company moved to the south side of Dublin Bay at Ringsend.

Locomotives Nos 133 and 186 are arriving into the 'Holyhead Yard' in North Wall, Dublin, with the 15.10 Adelaide (Belfast) liner train on Friday 22 August 1997. Included in the train's consist are four bogie fertiliser wagons, operated for the Richardson Fertiliser company. This stretch of line in the North Wall was originally the domain of the London & North Western Railway, who had their own terminus station for boat train traffic to and from Dublin City.

Newly painted locomotive No. 146 in IÉ livery is on pilot duties, seen shunting the Limerick liner at the 'Midland Yard' in North Wall on Tuesday 19 May 1998. In the background are the gantry cranes in the Holyhead Yard, which closed in January 2003. To the left of the cranes is the former train shed of the aforementioned L&NWR terminus, which closed in 1910 and is now demolished, although the station buildings which face the River Liffey remain to this day. This entire area is nowadays buried under the Spencer Dock Apartments.

'Shunting Pilot' locomotive No. 143, so proclaimed on its cabsides, discharges its duties at the 'Holyhead Yard' in North Wall, while 201 Class locomotive No. 205 waits to work the 13.00 Cork liner. Also visible is locomotive No. 154, which is waiting to depart with a Guinness keg transfer train to Heuston Goods. Across to the left in the Midland Yard, a rake of four-wheel timber wagons are stabled and in the far distance, a Dublin Pearse to Drogheda push-pull suburban service has just departed north from Connolly station on Monday 21 January 2002.

A Class locomotive No. 026 is departing North Wall with the 20.15 Dublin to Cork liner on the evening of Wednesday 12 June 1991. Behind the train can be seen Church Road signal cabin, which controlled a complex of junctions with the 'Liffey Branch', the Drumcondra to Glasnevin Junction line, as well as the connecting spur with the Dublin to Belfast main line. Church Road cabin was finally closed in 2015 during a rationalisation scheme of the North Wall area.

121 Class locomotives Nos 129 and 127 are preparing to depart from 'The Granaries' in North Wall, on their 135-mile-long journey to Sligo with the 14.50 laden Esso liner on Monday 9 October 1995. The final destination for this train will be the quayside freight yard in Sligo. 'The Granaries' is now the only surviving rail freight yard within North Wall. In the background can be seen the line leading towards the Alexandra Road tramway, where the railway gains entry into Dublin Port.

Locomotive No. 074 runs alongside the Royal Canal on the approach to Jones Road on the 'Liffey Branch' with the diverted 8.35 Sligo to Dublin Connolly passenger service on Sunday 2 February 1997. Note the trap points to the left of the train on the Down line, used to derail any offending vehicles descending the gradient towards North Wall. The buildings on the right occupy the site of the former Drumcondra Mill, which was served by a facing siding that had long since been removed by the time this scene was recorded.

Locomotive No. 021 is seen approaching North Strand Junction heading the 8.42 Marino Point to Shelton Abbey laden ammonia on Tuesday 10 March 1992. North Strand Junction is where the connecting freight-only line to North Wall via Church Road Junction diverges from the Drumcondra to Glasnevin Jct line.

NIR locomotive No. 8113 is way off its own territory in this shot at Drumcondra in Dublin's north inner city. Unlike sister locomotives Nos 8111 and 8112, which regularly worked freight south of the border, in later years No. 8113 was a rare visitor; she is seen here approaching Drumcondra with the 13.05 ex-Maynooth passenger service on Tuesday 16 November 1999.

Locomotive No. 8113 is again recorded in Dublin at Claude Road, just west of Drumcondra station, seen working the 14.00 empty Tullamore to Platin bulk cement train on Wednesday 8 October 2003. No. 8113 carries the name *Belfast & County Down*, in memory of one of the three larger railway companies to operate in Northern Ireland.

Locomotive No. 005 approaches Claude Road on Friday 8 May 1992 with an empty ballast train from Killucan, on the Sligo line, to Dublin's North Wall. Behind No. 005 is the vintage Great Southern & Western Railway-built plough van No. 8456, which was the oldest piece of rolling stock in operation on Irish Rail during the 1990s.

A panoramic 'bird's eye view' of the 13.00 North Wall to North Esk (Cork) liner train, seen approaching Glasnevin Junction with locomotive No. 074 at the helm on Monday 11 September 1995. This scene is recorded from the top of the silo located at the North City Mill. Immediately behind the train can be seen the footbridge at Claude Road from which the previous photos were recorded. In the far distance is Howth Head, located at the northern end of Dublin Bay.

Locomotive No. 077 heads past Glasnevin Junction with the 11.16 from Muine Bheag (Bagenalstown) to Dublin Connolly special, formed of the Mk III 'Cu Na Mara' International coach set, on Sunday 16 June 1996. In the foreground is the connection between the Drumcondra and Sligo lines, which converge with the 'Liffey Branch', whose tracks can just be glimpsed at the bottom of the photo. The playing pitches beyond the railway belong to St Vincent's school in Glasnevin, mentioned in the introductory text, where in my school days I first took note of the railway scene.

With the line towards Sligo diverging to the left, locomotives Nos 126 and 121 pass Glasnevin Junction with the 11.35 Cabra to Platin cement factory empty bulk cement train on Sunday 26 March 1995. The following day, locomotives Nos 126 and 121 worked the morning 5.30 empty gypsum to Kingscourt in County Cavan.

Locomotive No. 222 approaches Glasnevin Junction with the 8.42 Marino Point to Shelton Abbey laden ammonia train on Thursday 13 April 1995. With the withdrawal of the A Class locomotives after forty years' service, the 201 Class became firmly established on the ammonia workings. In the background can be seen the famous round tower of Glasnevin Cemetery, now recently restored.

Locomotive No. 082 catches the afternoon sun at Cabra in Dublin's northern suburbs with a 15.00 North Wall to Thurles fertiliser working on Saturday 1 October 1994. The sidings on the left serve the cement terminal at Cabra, which could accessed by a trailing connection just before the Fassaugh Road bridge in the distance.

Having earlier reversed in Dublin's North Wall following its arrival from Sligo on the 12.00 laden timber, locomotive No. 073 is recorded passing Cabra en route to stable overnight in the 'Heuston Goods' sidings on Saturday 16 August.2003. This train subsequently worked the 12.30 Heuston Goods to Waterford on Sunday the following day.

A busy scene at Cabra on Thursday 3 August 1995. Locomotive No. 217 passes with the 9.40 Shelton Abbey to Marino Point empty ammonia. Also at Cabra is locomotive No. 085, seen arriving with a second Cabra cement train from Platin. In the distance, sister locomotive No. 073 is about to depart with the 11.35 empty cement to Platin. At busy times, Cabra cement depot received two trains daily and twelve trains weekly, including Sundays. The cement depot finally closed on 11 December 1999.

Viewed from the old 'Military Platform' on a very hot July day at Heuston station (Tuesday 16 July 1996), locomotive No. 232 is ready to depart with the 17.20 to Cork. Beside No. 232 on Platform 2 is locomotive No. 071 standing at the head of the 17.30 Limerick to Ennis train, while over to the left the station inspector chats with a staff member. Up to the early twentieth century, the Military Platform was regularly used by troops travelling to and from the Curragh army camp base.

A panorama view of Heuston station (formerly Kingsbridge) on Friday 27 October 1995. Locomotive No. 155 is shunting Mk III coaches, while 'pilot' locomotive No. 176 sits in the background. Locomotive No. 230 is in Platform 1 with the 13.30 'Friday Only' to Cork, while sister locomotive No. 205 is in Platform 5. Behind No. 176 are two Mk III executive coaches and behind them are a rake of preserved coaches. The impressive building in the background is the former Great Southern & Western Railway goods office and is now the HQ of the Irish Railway Record Society, which houses the society's extensive library and archives of Irish railways.

Having emerged from the Phoenix Park tunnel and passed over the River Liffey, retro-liveried locomotive No. 071 passes Islandbridge Junction with the 11.05 North Wall to Thurles empty spoil train on Tuesday 18 October 2016. This is a popular location for rail enthusiasts and photographers overlooking Islandbridge Junction, where the line from Glasnevin Junction joins the Dublin to Cork main line.

Locomotive No. 082 is at journey's end passing Islandbridge on the approach to Heuston station with the morning 9.15 Galway to Dublin passenger service on Monday 21 May 2007. The disused building on the right overlooking the railway formerly belonged to the Islandbridge military barracks, which at the time of writing have recently been redeveloped into a residential apartment complex.

Locomotive No. 011 is pictured on the approach to Islandbridge Junction with the Saturday Limerick to North Wall laden barytes train. Although these wagons were primarily used on the ore traffic from Silvermines, at weekends they were regularly utilised for engineering works. On this occasion the wagons are seen laden with ballast on Saturday 4 April 1992 for weekend works in the Dublin area. The signal gantry visible above the train was known as the 'Bridge of Signals' and dated from the 1938 re-signalling scheme. To the right is the N4 dual carriageway, which leads west out of Dublin.

An early morning view of locomotives Nos 192 and 181 at Islandbridge on the approach to Dublin Heuston with an ex-Claremorris empty keg train at 7:00 on Thursday 15 June 2006. The cutting through which the railway passes at Islandbridge has for generations been known as 'The Gullet'.

Looking the opposite way from the previous scene (Thursday 15 June 2006), locomotives Nos 192 and 181 are recorded having entered the 'The Gullet'. The low sun is straight into my camera lens, but still makes a nice photograph. Nos 192 and 181 are blocked at the modern-day 'Bridge of Signals' as morning commuter trains get priority here. However, 201 Class locomotive No. 234 screams up the gradient out of Heuston with the 7.10 Dublin to Galway passenger service.

On Friday 30 June 2006, locomotive No. 219 takes its first trip out in its new 'Intercity' livery with the evening 20.20 Heuston Goods to Cork Guinness kegs liner. Visible at the rear of the train are two wheel-carrier wagons destined for Irish Rail's wagon workshops in Limerick and which will be later dropped off this train at Limerick Junction.

Locomotive No. 086 is hauling a failed 233 near journey's end at 'The Gullet' with the 6.45 Limerick to Heuston passenger service on Thursday 18 May 2006. The second last coach on this train of Mark IIs is in the refurbished livery, of which a uniform set was originally introduced for the Galway line services.

Locomotive No. 077 in its new 'battleship grey' livery with its EU regulatory number (0117077) is passing Cherry Orchard on the Up Slow line with an empty ballast train (HOBS) from Ballyhaunis to North Wall on Friday 19 July 2013. The station on the horizon is the new Part West & Cherry Orchard, which opened on 28 July 2008. This new station replacing an older station that had originally opened in May 1994 at the location photographed, but which closed when the quadruple tracks were installed under the Kildare Route Project in 2008.

Locomotive No. 148 passes through the original Clondalkin station with the Claremorris to North Wall empty Esso liner on Saturday 29 September 2001. Not a trace of this station remains today, as it too closed permanently in 2008 and was subsequently demolished and buried underneath four-track installations.

Locomotive No. 073 heads a Shelton Abbey to Thurles laden fertiliser through Newbridge on Thursday 10 July 1997. In later years, a bay platform was installed here on the Down side of the station to facilitate terminating commuter trains from Dublin.

Locomotives Nos 128 and 129 haul the 8.05 Waterford to North Wall 'Andrew Weir Shipping' (AWS) liner train out of the loop at the south end of Hazelhatch station on Monday 17 May 1999. This loop was installed as part of the Centralised Traffic Control signalling scheme of 1976. Nowadays the four tracks from Dublin converge into conventional Up and Down lines at this point beyond the now heavily rebuilt station at Hazelhatch.

Locomotive No. 212 is north of Sallins at Milepost 17 with the 7.00 Cork to Dublin Heuston passenger service on Wednesday 31 May 2006. Locomotive No. 212 entered traffic on Irish Rail in October 1994 and, like her other sisters, is named after an Irish river, No. 212 being allocated the name *River Slaney / Abhainn na Slaine*.

Not a train I expected to see at Sallins on 'Derby Sunday' – it completely took me by surprise; the 9.40 ex-Shelton Abbey empty ammonia, which usually ran on Sunday, was cancelled and instead a laden fertiliser with A Class locomotive No. 049 in charge ran in the booked path from Shelton Abbey to Thurles. Needless to say, I was pleasantly surprised and very pleased with this capture. When this view was recorded on 27 June 1993, Sallins station had not seen regular passenger workings since 1947.

On Friday 15 April 2005, 'Enterprise'-liveried locomotive No. 8208 catches a burst of sunlight on the approach to Sallins with the 11.45 North Wall to North Esk (Cork) liner, which consisted of the container pocket wagons (CPW). The CPWs entered traffic in 2002 and in later years saw use on DFDS and IWT liner trains. At the time of writing in April 2019, they are not presently restored to operate on any liner workings.

A pair of heavily weathered 121 Class locomotives, Nos 135 and 134, storm through the then recently reopened station at Sallins with the 15.30 Heuston Goods to Cork Guinness kegs on Saturday 4 June 1994. In the background on the Up line is another loop installed at the time of the CTC signalling scheme in 1976. The green fields seen behind the train have since been covered over by a new residential complex.

Locomotive No. 202 speeds through Newbridge with the 17.05 Heuston to Ennis passenger service on Saturday 14 April 2007. The first Mk III carriage behind the electric generator van (EGV) carries Irish Rail's 'City Gold' branding, effectively a coach for First Class paying passengers. The new bay platform for terminating commuter services is visible to the right.

Kildare on Saturday 23 May 1992 sees A Class locomotive No. 005 stopped in 'middle road' at the station with the 15.00 North Wall to Waterford Bell liner. This middle track in the station, a rare feature on Irish railways, is frequently used by non-stopping trains as well as freight workings requiring a reversal of their journeys to and from the Waterford line.

Locomotive No. 080 is pictured in the middle road at Kildare with a 13.00 North Wall to Cork 'airbrake liner' on Saturday 23 May 1992. A couple of engineering vehicles are seen stabled in the former goods yard to the right of the picture, this site being nowadays occupied by a track machine maintenance depot.

NIR locomotive No. 8113 makes a rare working on the sugar beet, seen here coming off the Waterford line at Cherryville Junction with the 7.45 diverted laden beet from Waterford to Mallow on Saturday 11 October 2003. The 2003 beet campaign was diverted to work via Kildare due to the Cahir Viaduct collapse, caused by a cement train, which occurred at the start of the campaign on Tuesday 7 October 2003.

Locomotive No. 212 heads across the viaduct at Monasterevin, which spans the River Barrow, with the 7.00 North Wall to Cork bulk cement on Saturday 18 October 2003. The first batch of these four-wheel bulk cement wagons (nicknamed 'bubbles') entered traffic on CIÉ in 1964 and remained in use until the complete cessation of rail-borne cement traffic in 2009. In the foreground is the Grand Canal.

Locomotive No. 218 is recorded approaching Portarlington with the 14.00 North Wall to Portlaoise 'Avonmore' laden grain train on Wednesday 20 September 1995. This grain traffic also operated from Waterford and Foynes and consisted of 20-foot containers with tarpaulin coverings, the same consist as the diverted Tara mines ore workings to Arklow.

Locomotive No. 203 stands at Portarlington with the 9.40 Shelton Abbey to Marino Point empty ammonia following a crossing and crew change with the 8.42 Marino Point to Shelton Abbey laden ammonia, which is worked by sister locomotive No. 222, on Wednesday 20 September 1995. Each of the trains demonstrates the method of ammonia train workings with a barrier wagon, complete with water-tank, marshalled at the front and rear.

Locomotive No. 076, hauling a failed No. 077, approaches Portarlington with the 11.00 Mallow to Portarlington laden spoil (train code W211) on Thursday 6 December 2018. The train had departed Cork on Tuesday 4 December with No. 077, but this locomotive failed outside Cork. In the background, the single-track branch to Athlone (the main line to Galway) diverges sharply away in a north-westerly direction towards Tullamore.

In glorious sunshine on the morning of Saturday 8 May 1993, locomotive No. 048 heads through Ballybrophy with the 7.50 Limerick to Inchicore empty barytes for overnight engineering works in the Dublin area. This train would usually return to Limerick on the Sunday for Monday morning Silvermines barytes ore working. Ballybrophy is the junction for the branch line to Limerick via Nenagh.

141 Class locomotives Nos 152 and 155 head south away from Limerick Junction with the 11.45 Waterford to Mallow laden beet on Saturday 28 November 1998. A rake of bagged cement, kegs and fertiliser wagons is parked in the southern yard, which nowadays is occupied by the station car park. In the background on the Down side of the line is Limerick Junction South signal cabin.

A Class locomotive No. 047 passes Knocklong with the 9.45 Waterford to Mallow laden beet on a wet Friday 23 October 1992. Knocklong station closed in 1977 and the signal cabin was dispensed with in 1988 when the line was re-signalled under Centralised Traffic Control.

A rather grubby-looking A Class locomotive No. 031 is photographed in Cork (Kent station) shunting the stock of the 15.10 Cork to Tralee passenger on Saturday 20 October 1990, which is comprised of 1960s-era Craven coaches and a Mk I GSV. The semaphores visible in this scene were replaced by colour-light signals in November 2018, which finally brought an end to mechanical signalling in the Cork area.

121 Class locomotives Nos 124 and 187 are photographed in the freight yard opposite Cork (Kent) station while discharging a bulk cement train formed of the air-braked bogie tank wagons on Saturday 29 May 2004. These bogie wagons entered service in 1979 and were placed into store in 2009 following the end of rail-borne cement trains.

With the final wagons at the rear of the train being loaded, locomotives Nos 129 and 135 stand in the goods siding at Millstreet with the 17.00 timber train to Waterford, formed of the four-wheel timber wagons, on Saturday 10 June 2000. By the year 2000, Millstreet no longer possessed a run-round loop, the train having to travel west to Rathmore to run round before returning through Millstreet en route to Mallow and Waterford.

Photographed at the east end of Banteer station on Saturday 10 May 1997, locomotive No. 164 is seen stabled adjacent to the old goods yard with a rake of ballast hoppers. This siding remains at Banteer for the purpose of loading ballast trains working on the Mallow–Killarney–Tralee line.

Locomotive No. 169 heads through Farranfore with the 19.00 Tralee to Limerick empty bag cement train on the evening of Saturday 24 May 1997. The signalman is about to hand the driver the token for the Farranfore–Killarney ETS section. Farranfore formerly had a private siding for handling fertiliser traffic. The station was also once the junction for the very scenic Valentia Harbour branch line, which regrettably closed in 1960.

Locomotive No. 025 enters the station at Askeaton with the 13.30 Foynes to Limerick empty barytes ore on Tuesday 20 August 1991. Note the Great Southern Railways era bilingual nameboard on the platform. This barytes traffic from the mines at Silvermines ceased in November 1993. In addition to the ore trains on this branch, there was also the coal and oil traffic for Asahi in Killala, County Mayo, which ceased in November 1997. The branch, however, continued to see grain, fertiliser and molasses trains, but the last revenue-earning train ran to Foynes in 2000.

Locomotive No. 152 heads gingerly through the forlorn-looking station at Ballingrane on the Foynes branch with the annual weedsprayer train on Tuesday 29 May 2001. Ballingrane was originally the junction for Foynes until the main route to Tralee via Newcastle West closed in 1975, a case of the branch outliving the main line. The overgrown signal cabin on the right closed in 1988 when Ballingrane ceased completely to be a junction following the disconnection and lifting of the disused Tralee line.

141 Class locomotive No. 154 is at Adare with the last weedsprayer train on the Foynes branch on Tuesday 7 May 2002. This was the last train to run over the Foynes branch. The station at Adare lost its passenger service in 1963 and closed completely to goods traffic in 1975.

A Class locomotive No. 014 pauses at Moate, County Westmeath, with the 15.40 Ballina to Dublin Connolly passenger service on Bank Holiday Monday 3 June 1985. By 1985, this former main line to Galway and west via the Mullingar–Athlone route had lost most of its passenger services, the majority of Galway and western line workings having been transferred to Dublin Heuston to operate via the Portarlington to Athlone line since 1973.

Locomotives Nos 135 and 188 arrive into Moate with the 7.15 Ballina to Dublin Connolly GAA special on 'All Ireland Sunday' on 17 September 1989. This section of the old Mullingar to Athlone line is now a public greenway used by cyclists and walkers, the line having seen little regular use by trains from the early 2000s onward.

This scene at Ballinalose sees locomotives Nos 135 and 128 heading through the station with an Athenry to Platin empty bulk cement working on Monday 2 April 2001. Since this view was recorded, the Down platform on the left is now disused, having been replaced by a brand new platform beyond the old goods shed, giving the station a 'staggered' platform layout.

Locomotive No. 216 moves away from the wayside station at Woodlawn while working the 11.00 Dublin Heuston to Galway passenger service on Saturday 8 April 1995. Locomotive No. 216, named *River Dodder / Abhainn na Dothra*, is now currently in the navy livery of the Belmond Grand Hibernian train, which began operating on Irish railways in 2016.

Framed by the semaphore signals in Galway, locomotive No. 087 is pictured shunting laden timber wagons for the 16.30 Galway to Waterford timber train on Monday 19 October 1998. The bridge in the foreground takes the railway across Lough Atalia, which overlooks Galway Bay. Visible above the train shed of the Galway station terminus is the former Midland Great Western's railway hotel.

Locomotives Nos 132 and 134 are stabled on Galway turntable waiting to couple up to their train, while 071 Class locomotive No. 075 prepares to depart with the 15.00 to Dublin Heuston on Bank Holiday Monday 1 June 1992. A solitary fuel tank wagon sits on the stub of the former Clifden branch. The Clifden branch operated for just forty years, from 1895 to April 1935. Galway Bay dominates the horizon.

Locomotive No. 141 leads classmate No. 151 on the approach to Ballyglunin on the Western Rail Corridor (WCR) with the Foynes to Ballina 'coal and oil' train on Monday 28 July 1997. By the mid-1990s this working, which was synonymous with the 'freight-only' Limerick–Athenry–Claremorris line, had been reduced to coal only, as depicted in this view.

Another view of locomotives Nos 141 and 151 heading the Foynes to Ballina Asahi coal and oil train on Monday 28 July 1997, again on the WRC but passing the closed station at Ballindine. This traffic ceased in November 1997 when the textile plant of Asahi Ltd at Killala, County Mayo, closed.

Locomotives Nos 173 and 141 pass through the station at Tuam on Saturday 8 November 1997 with the Irish Traction Group's 'Western Venturer' rail tour. For its return journey, this rail tour was diverted via Tuam on the WRC due to a serious derailment at Knockcroghery in County Roscommon on the Claremorris to Athlone line, making this rail tour the last passenger train to date to operate over the now-closed Athenry to Claremorris section on the Western Rail Corridor.

Locomotives Nos 133 and 182 enter the then closed station at Gort on the Western Rail Corridor with a photographic 'run pass' while working the Irish Railway Record Society's annual 'Executive Mk III' rail tour on a sunny Saturday 31 May 1997. As the name implies, this society was established in 1946 for the purpose of recording and preserving the historical records of Ireland's railways, which is achieved through its library and archives at Heuston station, Dublin.

Entering traffic with CIÉ in November 1966, 181 Class locomotive No. 187 heads south through Gort en route from Claremorris to Limerick with the annual weedsprayer train on Thursday 29 May 1997. Having originally closed to regular passenger traffic in 1976, the station at Gort has since been reopened for the Limerick–Galway services, which commenced operation on 29 March 2010.

Locomotives Nos 184 and 172 are pictured in the cement siding at Tullamore while discharging a bulk cement train on Friday 18 April 2003. Upon completion of discharging, the train will depart in its booked path (the 14.00 Tullamore to North Wall) and later work forward to Platin cement factory near Drogheda. Note the vents on the front cab of locomotive No. 184, a feature which distinguished the 181 Class fleet from their older 141 classmates, which dated from 1962.

'Enterprise' locomotive No. 209 approaches Commons Bridge on the Athlone line just outside the town of Portarlington with the 13.55 Tullamore to Platin empty bulk cement on Saturday 15 February 2003. The train is passing over the bridge spanning the River Barrow, which marks the county boundary between Offaly and Laois.

071 Class locomotive No. 077 heads east through Clara with the 8.05 Ballina to Waterford 'Norfolk Liner' train on Saturday 3 April 2004. Note the steam-age water column still in situ between the running lines. Although possessing a passing loop, Clara has only one passenger platform, an indication of the Athlone–Portarlington line's original branch line status. After 1973, the majority of main line trains to Galway and the west were diverted via this route.

Locomotive No. 077 arrives at Roscommon with the 15.30 Westport to Dublin Heuston passenger service on Sunday 1 April 2007. The signalman on the platform is about to hand the driver the ETS token for the section to Knockcroghery. Mechanical signalling on the Mayo line was replaced by Centralised Traffic Control in 2007 and this saw the closure of the distinctive tall Roscommon signal cabin and the removal of the semaphore signals. Note the soon-to-be commissioned automatic lights and barriers for the station level crossing.

Locomotive No. 080 departing Claremorris with the 13.30 Westport to Dublin Heuston passenger service on Friday 17 May 1991. The Athenry to Tuam line converges from the left and last saw rail movement in 2006 when a PWD inspection car traversed the disused route to Athenry. Of the original five lines radiating out from the town of Claremorris, only the through east–west main line remains in use today. Apart from the disused line to Athenry, the other two routes that have closed are the Ballinrobe branch (in 1959) and the line to Collooney (in 1975), although the tracks on the latter route remain in situ, albeit rusty and overgrown.

141 Class locomotives Nos 162 and 152 prepare to leave Ballina with the 16.45 Ballina to Waterford laden timber on the evening of Monday 7 March 2005. Despite the network-wide decline in rail freight traffic, the yard at Ballina on the left receives daily liner and timber trains to this day.

On Friday 28 April 1995, Class leader locomotive No. 071 was recorded at the Deep Water Quay in Sligo working a bitumen tar transfer from Cold Chon Ltd to Sligo Yard. This section of the quay was re-laid to take the weight of the heavy 071 Class. No. 071 worked the passenger from Dublin Connolly that morning, and on completion of its shunting duties at Sligo Quay, the locomotive worked the 13.25 passenger back to Dublin Connolly. The track on the Deep Water Quay was lifted in 2002 following the cessation of the Cold Chon traffic.

On a damp day, locomotive No. 072 departs on the steep gradient from Sligo Quay with the 12.00 Sligo Quay to Waterford laden timber train, consisting of the four-wheel wagons, on Saturday 10 July 1999. Shrouded in mist and cloud on the horizon is the Dartry mountain range, which encompasses Cope's Mountain, Kings Mountain and the distinctive flat-top mountain known as Ben Bulben. The timber traffic from Sligo ceased in 2008, but there remains hope that this freight flow will return in the future, bringing back a welcome return of loco-hauled trains on this scenic line.

A panoramic view of Sligo Quay freight yard and Sligo town beyond, with locomotive No. 075 shunting the Waterford-bound timber train in the yard prior to departure on Monday 9 March 1998. Note the steam-age water column, still in situ. This view is recorded from the container gantry crane, which remains in situ but disused.

Metrovick A Class locomotive No. 038 is working hard past Ballymote with the 5.20 North Wall to Sligo Quay laden Esso liner on Thursday 29 July 1993. The signal cabin and goods store have all been demolished at this location. Evidence of the recently lifted loop can still be seen in this photograph, Ballymote having ceased to be a block-post when the signal cabin closed in January 1989. Visible in the left background of this scene is Ballymote Castle, built around AD 1300.

Prior to entering service, a four-car 2700 Class railcar set consisting of Nos 2701, 2702, 2704 and 2703 is seen while on trial at Edgeworthstown on Saturday 18 July 1998. This location has invariably been named as either Mostrim or Edgeworthstown, the latter name derived from nineteenth-century resident and author Maria Edgeworth. The railcar sets are depicted in their original black and orange livery with 'Arrow' branding, which was later superseded by the 'Commuter' brand colours of blue and green.

Locomotive No. 088 gives out a blast of black exhaust smoke as it powers through Edgeworthstown, heading the 12.00 Sligo timber train to Waterford on Saturday 5 June 2004. Since this view has been recorded, the Midland Great Western Railway-style signal cabin has been closed and demolished (the latter action to facilitate platform extensions).

With the driver about to exchange the ETS token, Northern Ireland Railway's locomotive No. 112, named *Northern Counties*, enters Enfield on a sunny evening with the 19.40 North Wall to Sligo Quay liner, consisting on this occasion of 40-foot containers and kegs on Monday 21 July 1997.

A Class locomotive No. 023 heads past the signal cabin and level crossing at Clonsilla with the 14.50 North Wall to Sligo Quay laden Esso liner on Wednesday 26 September 1990. Although Clonsilla has been re-signalled since 2000, when the former double-track line was reinstated to Maynooth, the cabin is still retained as a gate-post, being one of the last still to be equipped with a hand-operated gate-wheel for level crossing gates.

A Class locomotive No. 005 stands basking in the evening sunshine at Clonsilla with the 20.10 North Wall to Sligo Quay liner train, which was waiting to cross the Up Sligo passenger on Tuesday 22 June 1993. This locomotive originally entered CIÉ traffic as 'A5' in November 1955 and was re-engined with a GM power-plant in 1971; it was withdrawn twenty-four years later in March 1995.

NIR locomotive No. 112 has just passed the level crossing at Porterstown between Coolmine and Clonsilla with the 8.30 Sligo to Dublin Connolly passenger service on Sunday 28 September 2003. The distinctive tall building in the background is the old Porterstown school house, dating from 1854, which remained in use as a national school until 1963. Hidden by trees on the right, the Royal Canal parallels the railway line towards Dublin.

On the evening of Monday 14 June 2004, locomotive No. 075 crosses the M50 motorway with the 19.20 North Wall to Sligo Quay liner, its load comprising a mix of Guinness kegs and laden Esso tankers on the rear. This bridge carries the Sligo line over the M50 motorway, the M50 being the primary orbital ring road around the city of Dublin, which opened in the mid-1990s. The old stone-arched bridge visible in the background takes a pathway across the adjacent Royal Canal.

141 Class locomotives Nos 143 and 151 are pictured passing the station at Ashtown in west Dublin with the 7.30 Sligo to Dublin Connolly passenger service on Monday 25 July 1988. After many years of not receiving any regular stopping service, Ashtown was reopened in 1982, and at the time of writing it still has a manned, operated, gated level crossing. Visible to the far right is the lock-keeper's house for the tenth lock on the Royal Canal.

In the late 1980s and early 1990s, Irish Rail leased rolling stock from Northern Ireland Railways, which comprised three 80 Class railcar sets (numbers 68, 69 and 86) for Connolly–Maynooth and Cork–Cobh commuter services, as well as the Bray–Greystones shuttle. Railcar set 86, with IR branding, is passing Liffey Junction with the 16.10 Dublin Connolly to Maynooth service on Thursday 12 July 1990. Visible in the background is Liffey Junction signal cabin, which closed in July 1991.

One of my favourite freight flows, maybe because it only ran in the hours of darkness, but that all changed in 1988; from 22.00 out of Dublin's North Wall, it was switched to 14.50 in the afternoon. In this scene dating from Monday 2 September 1991, sitting at the trackside with the sun on my back, I could hear it cranking up out of North Wall, via Newcomen Bridge, with A Class locomotive No. 021 heading the laden Esso liner for Sligo on the hard rising gradient on the approach to Liffey Junction. To the right of the train, a long siding ran parallel alongside the main line from Liffey Junction to the North City Mills at Glasnevin, which closed in 1973 and was lifted in 1977. Viewed from my classroom at Glasevin in the early 1960s, this was the siding that I remember seeing trains operating on.

Class leader locomotive No. 001 is passing the seventh lock on the Royal Canal at Liffey Junction with a colourful 23.00 Sligo Quay to North Wall liner train near journey's end on Thursday 6 August 1992. Liffey Junction was the junction for the former main line into the Dublin terminus of Broadstone, which closed to passengers in 1937. Following the abolition of Broadstone steam shed in 1962, the line survived as a siding into the early 1970s, the stub being latterly retained for storing redundant rolling stock. The Broadstone line has since reopened as a Luas tramway in December 2017.

NIR 80 Class railcar No. 86 arrives at Broombridge station on its opening day on Monday 2 July 1990. In addition to the Luas line into Dublin City, a new tram depot has since been built to the right behind the station, which opened in 2017. Note the tall bracket-style signal on the Up line, which possesses just one semaphore; formerly this bracket featured a second signal indicating the divergence of the Broadstone line. The land to the right was formerly occupied by a cattle bank served by sidings.

With a friendly wave from the train guard, a fresh-looking 141 Class locomotive No. 143 passes the disused platforms at Liffey Junction sporting its new IR livery while working an engineers' materials train from Enfield to North Wall on Sunday 6 January 1991, comprising six empty bogie flat wagons.

Approaching Broombridge from the west is locomotive No. 082 heading the 10.05 Maynooth to Dublin Connolly passenger service on a snowy Thursday 1 March 2001. Nowadays the background scene at this location is dominated by a new road bridge spanning both the railway and the Royal Canal. This new bridge replaced Reilly's level crossing in 2015, which up to closure was still a manually operated crossing with gates.

Guinness-liveried DART sets Nos 8320, 8120, 8325 and 8125 are approaching Cosh level crossing on the Howth Branch with a Howth to Bray service on Tuesday 28 January 1997. The Guinness brand was the first to advertise on the exterior of the DART trains, and since then, Emirates airlines have also now featured. In the far distance to the left of the photo is Ireland's Eye, situated directly north of Howth Harbour.

With the station of Sutton & Baldoyle visible in the distance, locomotive No. 081 stands on the Down line at Cosh level crossing on the Howth Branch while unloading track panels for relaying work on Saturday 22 February 2003. The Howth branch was electrified as part of the DART scheme in 1984 and nowadays seldom sees locomotive-hauled trains, these usually being PWD or rail tour operations.

121 Class locomotive No. 130 has arrived at Sutton & Baldoyle with a Mk III push-pull train to Howth comprised of set Nos 6310 and 6105, substituting on a passenger service in the absence of the electrified DART trains due to engineering works on Sunday 7 April 1991. It was between 1988 and 1989, that some of the 121 Class locomotives were equipped for push-pull operation with then new Mk III push-pull stock. To the left beneath the platform awning can be seen my two daughters Siobhán and Deirdre, along with my fellow railway photographer and friend Richard Wall.

On the afternoon of Friday 9 June 1995, Class leader No. 121, with sister locomotive No. 124, enter Malahide with the 16.12 Mosney to Dublin Connolly passenger service prior to the extension of the electrified DART services to this popular seaside town. DART services were extended from Howth Junction to Malahide in April 2000. To the left, beyond the Down platform, is the disused Great Northern Railway (Ireland)-style signal cabin, which is preserved to this day. In the distance, the line stretches north across the Broadmeadow Estuary towards Donabate.

201 Class No. 215 passes through Malahide station with the Belfast Central to Dublin Connolly 'Enterprise' service consisting of NIR Mk II stock on Wednesday 6 August 1997. In this scene, the platforms have been resurfaced and extended in preparation for the electrified DART services. This view nowadays is no longer possible due to the presence of the overhead line equipment, which extends out towards the estuary and stops short of the Broadmeadow Viaduct.

Locomotive No. 208, in the then new 'Enterprise' livery, speeds through the station at Donabate on the 15.00 Belfast Central to Dublin Connolly 'Enterprise' on Monday 21 July 1997. The train is comprised of a NIR Mk II set, which would shortly be replaced on these trains by the introduction of the French-built De Dietrich coaches.

On Wednesday 28 June 1995, locomotive No. 209 passes the redundant GNR(I)-era signal cabin at the north end of Donabate station with the 15.00 Belfast Central to Dublin Connolly 'Enterprise', while an empty bulk cement train heads north for Platin cement factory. The original Northern Ireland Railway's blue livery aesthetically suited the company's two 201 Class locomotives (Nos 208 and 209), which were named *River Lagan* and *River Foyle* respectively.

141 Class locomotives Nos 164 and 175 lead the 17.00 Dublin North Wall to Platin combined empty bulk and bag cement train past Rogerstown Estuary, between Donabate and Rush & Lusk, on the evening of Thursday 3 August 1995. Locomotives Nos 164 and 175 each show the old and new corporate liveries of Iarnród Éireann, featuring the older 'IR Point' and newer 'Plug & Socket' logos.

201 Class locomotive No. 217 approaches Rush & Lusk with the 9.20 North Wall to Belfast Adelaide liner on the morning of Wednesday 28 June 1995. The two houses behind the signal cabin have since been demolished and the area turned into a station car park. The cabin was dispensed with in May 1994 following the extension of Centralised Traffic Control signalling between Malahide and Drogheda.

With the station's GNR(I)-style Up Starting semaphore showing clear, locomotives Nos 170 and 165 head through Rush & Lusk with the 15.00 Belfast to Dublin Connolly 'Enterprise' on Sunday 11 September 1988. Rush signal cabin had an eleven-lever McKenzie & Holland-manufactured frame and was typical of the style found on the ex-Great Northern system. In the background, a CIÉ KD Class Bombardier bus is seen in the station forecourt awaiting its next turn of duty.

Pictured just north of Rush & Lusk at Ratharton Bridge on Thursday 27 May 1999, 121 Class locomotives Nos 128 and 129 are seen leading the 10.45 Kingscourt to North Wall laden gypsum train, which will work beyond Dublin to the Castlemungret cement factory outside Limerick. Delivered in 1961, the 121 Class originally operated 'bonnet-first' while on trial, but following visibility concerns they were then operated cab-first. Between 1973 and 1975, the 121 fleet were equipped for multiple operation, either paired with a classmate, as demonstrated in this scene at Ratharton Bridge, or with another 141 or 181 Class locomotive.

141 Class locomotive No. 156 arrives at Skerries on Wednesday 5 July 1989 with a Drogheda to Dublin Pearse suburban commuter service. Note the turned up headlight on locomotive No. 156, which acted as an aid for British Army helicopters when tracking cross-border freight trains during the Northern Ireland 'Troubles'. Note the signalman's bike beneath signal cabin. The cabin itself closed in May 1994 with the Great Northern Line re-signalling, but remains in situ today.

NIR locomotive No. 208 approaches Skerries station with the 8.00 Belfast Central to Dublin Connolly 'Enterprise' on the morning of Thursday 22 June 1995. Just three months previously, locomotive No. 208 had arrived into Dublin Port by ship from London, Ontario, Canada, on Saturday 25 March 1995. The siding in the foreground formerly served the goods yard but is nowadays used for storing engineering vehicles.

141 Class locomotive No. 173 pulls the 16.52 Dublin Pearse to Drogheda commuter service out of Skerries station on the evening of Tuesday 28 August 1990. The generator steam van (GSV) behind the locomotive belonged to a fleet of five 'Dutch' vans, so named because of the design style of their body and bogies (the latter supplied by Werkspoor of Utrecht). They were built in 1969 at Dundalk Engineering Works. In the background to the left is the typical GNR(I)-style stationmaster's house.

With the town of Skerries in the background, A Class locomotive No. 051 heads north past the old-style GNR(I) 'Up Distant' semaphore signal for Skerries with an empty Tara mines ore train on Friday 10 August 1990. As part of the 1990s infrastructure upgrade on the Dublin to Belfast main line, the Down track has been recently re-laid with modern concrete sleepers and long welded rails, while the Up line awaits similar treatment.

A Class locomotive No. 011 enters Balbriggan with a rake of 'bubble' wagons as it works the 11.35 Cabra to Platin empty bulk cement train on Tuesday 13 June 1989. The train has just passed over a stone-built viaduct which overlooks the small inner harbour at this seaside town.

The Metrovick A Class leader, locomotive No. 001, is recorded passing Balbriggan with the 10.20 Tara mines to Alexandra Road laden ore train on Tuesday 21 September 1993. No. 001 entered traffic on CIÉ as 'A1'. Its 1,200 hp Crossley engine was replaced by a 1,325 hp General Motors power-plant in March 1971, and survived in service until withdrawal in September 1995. Balbriggan signal cabin, visible in the background, was demolished in May 2000 having been closed six years previously.

121 Class locomotive No. 130 is crossing Gormanston Viaduct with the 16.26 Dublin Pearse to Drogheda commuter service on the evening of Saturday 10 September 1994. The train is formed of a Mk III push-pull set, which the 121 Class fleet solely operated on until the arrival of the push-pull-equipped 201 Class fleet in 1995. This viaduct, located just south of Gormanston station, crosses the River Delvin and marks the boundary between the counties of Dublin and Meath.

By early 1995, the sight of A Class locomotives working the Tara mines ore trains was in its final weeks, this being one of the last dedicated duties for these Metrovick locomotives, the last honours falling to locomotives Nos 012 and 015. The latter engine is seen approaching Gormanston in low winter sun with the morning 9.50 Navan (Tara mines) to Alexandra Road laden ore on Friday 6 January 1995. Within weeks the A Class were gone from these trains, having been replaced by the 071 Class locomotives, and so ended an era and another began.

181 Class locomotive No. 185 is passing Gormanston with the 11.35 Belfast Adelaide to Dublin North Wall 'Richardsons Fertiliser' on Saturday 10 September 1994. In the distance, a 2600 Class 'Arrow' railcar heads north to Drogheda. Gormanston signal cabin, prominent in these views, is now preserved on the Cavan & Leitrim Railway at Dromod, County Leitrim.

Belmond-liveried 201 Class locomotive No. 216 is recorded just south of Mosney with the 8.20 Dundalk to Dublin Connolly Belmond 'Grand Hibernian' train of refurbished Mk III stock on Sunday 14 May 2017. Launched in August 2016 with a target market of tourists visiting Ireland, the 'Grand Hibernian' train travels throughout the country, visiting Cork, Killarney, Galway, Westport, Dublin and Belfast. The train facilities includes sleeping accommodation, a restaurant, a bar and a library, as well as an observation car.

Viewed from the single platform at Mosney, A Class locomotive No. 049 passes with the 13.20 Navan to Dublin Pearse laden zinc ore train from Tara mines, en route to Arklow on Wednesday 15 July 1992. This train would be stabled overnight in the 'Boston Sidings' south of Pearse station in Dublin, before continuing its journey to Arklow, the zinc being exported by ship from the port of Arklow.

The attractive GNR(I) signal cabin at Laytown slumbers, the block-post having been 'switched out' for the afternoon, as locomotive No. 011 powers through the station with the 13.20 Navan to Alexandra Road (Dublin Port) laden Tara mines ore train on Wednesday 16 March 1994. As with the other signal cabins located between Malahide and Drogheda, Laytown cabin closed in May 1994 and has since been demolished.

On Wednesday 19 March 1997, locomotive No. 209 is pushing with driving van trailer No. 9002 on the front, seen departing Drogheda on the 11.10 Belfast Central to Dublin Connolly 'De Dietrich' trial train prior to entering service. During this period, Drogheda station was undergoing extensive engineering works, with platform realignments and the removal of the middle-road track. The freight-only branch line from Navan and Kingscourt converges from the right just beyond the platforms.

In pre-De Dietrich stock days, NIR locomotive No. 208 crosses over onto the Up line as it departs south from Drogheda with the 10.00 Belfast Central to Dublin Connolly 'Enterprise' on Sunday 15 September 1996. Nowadays the site to the right is occupied by the Drogheda Railcar Maintenance Depot, which opened in 2003.

Viewed from Buckies Bridge, ex-works NIR locomotive No. 111, named *Great Northern*, approaches Drogheda station from the south with the 13.00 Dublin Connolly to Belfast Central 'Enterprise' on Monday 27 March 1995. Locomotive No. 111 was one of three General Motors diesels supplied to NIR in the early 1980s, Nos 111 and 112 entering service in February 1981, while No. 113 arrived later in August 1984.

After the withdrawal of the Metrovick A Class in 1995 after forty years of service, the 141 and 181 Class diesels replaced the Metrovicks on the Kingscourt gypsum traffic. On Tuesday 4 June 1996, locomotives Nos 158 and 146 are at the 'dead-end' terminus at Kingscourt, County Cavan, with a laden gypsum train for Limerick cement factory. The branch from Navan to Kingscourt lost its passenger service in 1947, but remained in regular use for gypsum traffic until October 2001.

121 Class locomotives Nos 126 and 121 are passing the gypsum factory south of Kingscourt with the 10.45 Kingscourt to Platin laden gypsum on Monday 27 March 1995. A rarely used private siding once diverged to the left into the factory, the primary produce exported been paper, but it had fallen into disuse many years previously by the time this scene was recorded.

Recorded on the Kingscourt branch, A Class locomotive No. 002 passes through the disused and overgrown station at Nobber with the 10.45 Kingscourt to Platin laden gypsum on Wednesday 6 July 1988. This locomotive was another one of the CIÉ diesel fleet to be fitted with a modified upturned headlight for working cross-border freight trains. Visible in the background above the former goods shed is Nobber Motte, a one-time fortified mound dating from the twelfth century.

Locomotives Nos 185 and 168 are approaching the level crossing at Castletown on the Kingscourt branch with the 10.45 Kingscourt to Limerick laden gypsum train on Monday 27 March 2000. The Kingscourt branch was characterised by numerous gated level crossings, all of which had to be operated by the train guard. The approach to some of these crossings were guarded by fixed distant semaphore signals, many of which dated from the late nineteenth century, as exemplified by the ancient-looking signal visible in the background of this scene.

A Class locomotive No. 048 pauses at the old station at Wilkinstown with the Kingscourt to Platin laden gypsum on Monday 27 September 1993. There was an exception to the guard-operated crossings at Wilkinstown, where the resident lady gate-keeper regularly assisted the train crew by opening and closing the gates, as recorded in this scene.

Locomotives Nos 126 and 121 are pictured in the cutting on the approach to Tara Junction with the 10.45 Kingscourt to Platin laden gypsum on Monday 27 March 1995. Located west of the town of Navan, Tara Junction is the location where the Kingsbridge branch joined the former Great Northern Railway's branch line from Drogheda to Navan and Oldcastle, a junction being re-established here in 1977 when a mile-long section of the Navan to Oldcastle line was re-laid to serve the Tara mines facility.

The 181 Class locomotive leader with No. 155 enters the ex-Great Northern Railway station at Navan with the morning 9.20 laden Tara mines ore train to Alexandra Road (Dublin Port) on Friday 10 February 2006. Due to a failure of the usual 071 Class locomotive diagrammed on this train, locomotives Nos 181 and 155 deputised on the run between Navan and Drogheda. Navan lost its passenger service in 1958, but the station – with its single platform and GNR(I) style yellow-bricked building – survives, as does the signal cabin, the last such Great Northern cabin presently in use at the time of writing.

NIR locomotive No. 112 *Northern Counties* is near the site of the old GNR(I) halt at Lougher between Beauparc and Duleek on the Navan branch, with the 9.20 laden Tara mines ore train to Alexandra Road on Thursday 5 February 2004. The first and third ore wagons on this train have been converted from open-top shale wagons (used between Birdhill and Limerick), as identified by the waist-height rib on their bodysides.

Locomotive No. 036 is approaching the tall road overbridge at Kellystown with the 11.00 Belfast Central to Dublin Connolly 'Enterprise', formed of Irish Rail Mk II stock, on Monday 10 May 1993. Kellystown marks the gradient summit on this section of the Dublin to Belfast main line between Drogheda and Dundalk, featuring climbs between 1-in-160 and 1-in-200. A block-post was located here and was purported to feature Ireland's smallest signal cabin, the hut-like structure possessing just four levers, being used to split the long section between the cabins of Dunleer and Drogheda North. Kellystown cabin closed in August 1973.

A Class locomotive No. 051 is working hard past Dunleer with the 9.55 Belfast (Adelaide) to Platin cement factory (Drogheda) empty bulk cement train on Saturday 8 July 1989. Dunleer station closed in 1984 but there is pressure from the local population to reopen it. The signal cabin was on the Up side at the Drogheda end and is now demolished, having closed in 1997. This picture was taken from the station footbridge, which no longer exists.

A three-piece De Dietrich 'trial train', comprising driving van trailer Nos 9003, 9103 and 9209 with 'Enterprise' locomotive No. 206 pushing at the rear, is recorded just south of Dunleer on Wednesday 14 May 1997. Note the old-style Great Northern Railway (Ireland) semaphore signal, this being the 'Down Distant' signal for Dunleer. Dunleer and Poyntzpass were the last locations on the Dublin to Belfast main line to feature mechanical signalling until it was replaced by Centralised Traffic Control signalling in 1997.

Locomotive No. 164 is passing the disused platforms of the former Castlebellingham station with the combined 11.35 Belfast Adelaide and 14.00 ex-Dundalk Barrack Street liner train on Tuesday 4 October 1994. The Mourne Mountains of County Down in Northern Ireland provide a scenic backdrop. Castlebellingham closed completely in September 1976 and all the station buildings were demolished afterwards.

On Thursday 17 June 1993, NIR locomotive No. 113 *Belfast & County Down* has arrived into Dundalk with an engineers' train, to run round before departing back across the border while engaged in a track relaying job on the Down main line between the border and Newry in Northern Ireland. In the background can be seen Dundalk North signal cabin, formerly one of eight in the Dundalk area and which was demolished in 2002 to facilitate the construction of new railcar stabling sidings, the cabin having been largely redundant following the cessation of mechanical signalling at Dundalk in 1996. The track serving the goods yard in the foreground is nowadays a car park.

Locomotive No. 162 is recorded in the new Irish Rail livery at Dundalk with the 9.45 North Wall (Dublin) to Adelaide (Belfast) liner on Thursday 17 June 1993. En route this train had picked up six bulk cement wagons at Drogheda and is now waiting for a path over the border into Northern Ireland. Dundalk station features some of the best preserved examples of the Great Northern Railway's yellow-bricked buildings designed by that company's architect William Hemingway Mills. The site nowadays to the right is occupied by railcar stabling sidings.

201 Class locomotive No. 202 prepares to take the sharp curve at the south end of Poyntzpass station with the morning 9.55 Belfast Adelaide to Platin empty bulk cement train on Saturday 10 June 1995. Poyntzpass station was closed originally in 1965, but was reopened by NIR in 1984 to serve local trains between Portadown and Newry. The signal cabin, which controlled a nice collection of Great Northern Railway semaphore signals visible in this scene, was made redundant in 1997.

Locomotive No. 075 has navigated the curves at Poyntzpass with the 8.00 Dublin Connolly to Belfast Central 'Enterprise' service on Saturday 11 July 1987. Until the signal cabin closed in 1997, the level crossing gates were controlled by a hand-wheel in the cabin. The small village of Poyntzpass lies off to the right. The designation 'SA' beside the numerals on No. 075 indicates that the locomotive has been equipped with air-brakes.

Former CIE Metrovick locomotive No. 227, now renumbered as MV106, is pictured at Portadown while stabled on an engineers' train on Saturday 23 July 1994. The NIR 'MV' Class comprised six 1,100 hp locomotives purchased from CIE in the mid-1980s. These were the 550hp C Class engines built in 1956–57. To the left can be seen the brick base of the one-time Portadown Junction signal cabin, which formerly controlled the GNR(I) lines to Armagh and Derry, which were closed in 1957 and 1965 respectively.

In this scene dating from Friday 23 June 1999, locomotives Nos 126 and 142 are recorded passing Balmoral in Belfast's southern suburbs with the Dundalk to Belfast Adelaide empty Richardson Fertiliser train. Since 2002, no freight trains have operated to and from Northern Ireland. Adelaide freight yard itself has since been converted into a DMU maintenance depot.

Hunslet-built locomotive No. 102, named *Falcon*, is recorded on pilot duties at Adelaide Yard, Belfast, shunting a rake of fertiliser vans on Monday 24 June 1996. Locomotive No. 102 was one of three locomotives supplied by Hunslet to NIR, been built by BREL at Doncaster in 1970. They were designated as the 101 (DL) Class and were named *Eagle*, *Falcon* and *Merlin* respectively, these names been formerly carried by ex-GNR(I) V Class compound locomotives. Only No. 102 survived in traffic into the new millennium, being withdrawn in 2002, and is now preserved at the Ulster Folk & Transport Museum at Cultra.

NIR locomotive No. 208 approaches the station at Adelaide with the afternoon 15.00 Belfast Central to Dublin Connolly 'Enterprise' service on Saturday 14 October 1995. The long siding to the left was a spur off the freight yard and served the adjacent Guinness depot, the keg traffic having been the last freight-flow to be conveyed by rail from Belfast, which finally ceased in 2002. Adelaide freight depot was first opened in 1969, the site having been previously the primary GNR(I) locomotive shed in Belfast.

NIR 80 Class railcar No. 95 enters City Hospital with the 11.00 Derry/Londonderry to Belfast Central passenger service on Saturday 12 April 1997. Beyond the twin-arch bridge is the Black Mountain, with the BBC transmitter on its summit. City Hospital was opened in 1986 on the line of the former Belfast Central Railway, which was largely reinstated in 1976. This railway originally connected the Dublin to Belfast main line with the Belfast & County Down system, as well as the docks of Belfast and the lines serving north Ulster.

An attractive suburban-liveried NIR 80 Class railcar, No. 82 approaches Belfast Central with the 17.00 Bangor to Portadown commuter service on the evening of Saturday 16 June 1990. The train has just crossed the Lagan Viaduct and looming in the distance is the impressive Belfast landmark of the Harland & Wolff shipbuilding gantries at Queen's Island, these two gantry cranes being named *Samson* and *Goliath*. The train is passing the site of East Bridge Street Junction, where, until 1965, a branch line of the Belfast Central Railway diverged to the left to serve Belfast's docks, which also gave access to the city's other terminus of York Road.

HUNGARIAN RAILWAYS

DAVE SMITH│STEVE MADDEN